THE CLASSIC
CHRISTMAS
TREASURY
FOR CHILDREN

This book belongs to

_____

THE CLASSIC
CHRISTMAS TREASURY
FOR CHILDREN

Edited by
Louise Betts Egan

With Illustrations by
Andrew Babanovsky ❧ Nancy Carpenter
John Gurney ❧ Kay Life ❧ Scott Gustafson
Robyn Officer ❧ Karen Pritchett ❧ Erin Wise

Produced by Ariel Books

COURAGE
BOOKS
AN IMPRINT OF RUNNING PRESS
PHILADELPHIA • LONDON

10 9 8 7 6 5 4 3 2 1
Digit on the right indicates the number of this printing.

Library of Congress Cataloging-in-Publication Number 89-43004

ISBN 0-7624-0187-7

Printed in Singapore
Designed by Tilman Reitzle
Art direction by Armand Eisen

Published by Courage Books, an imprint of
Running Press Book Publishers
125 South Twenty-second Street
Philadelphia, Pennsylvania 19103-4399

CONTENTS

THE NUTCRACKER

Abridged and adapted from the story
by E.T.A. Hoffman

It was Christmas Eve at the Stahlbaum house, and it began in the grand, wonderful way the evening always had. The Christmas tree was resplendent with gold and silver apples, sugared almonds, flower-shaped chocolate bonbons, and hundreds of tiny candles that twinkled like stars. Beneath the tree were so many presents, anyone could guess that young Fritz and Marie Stahlbaum had been very good all year.

Fritz was playing with his new infantry of toy soldiers, and Marie was cradling her new, elegantly dressed doll, when in walked a most strange-looking man. He was short and thin, with skin as wrinkled as a prune, and he wore a black patch over one eye.

"Uncle Drosselmeier!" cried Fritz and Marie. They ran to greet the odd-looking man, who was a close, though rather mysterious, friend of the family.

"What have you brought us?" asked Fritz. Indeed, even the adults were curious, for Herr Drosselmeier's Christmas presents were always remarkable.

Herr Drosselmeier smiled and waited until he had everyone's attention. He then reached into his black cape and pulled out a

THE CLASSIC CHRISTMAS TREASURY

small wooden soldier. The soldier's head was much too big for his body, and he had a strange, flat sort of smile painted on his wooden face. His uniform was quite handsome—a scarlet coat with gold trim, pants to match, shiny black boots, and a bright, gold helmet.

"Look," said Herr Drosselmeier, "it's a nut-cracker!" He opened the soldier's mouth and placed a nut between its teeth. He pushed down the handle, and with a quick *crack!* the broken shell fell to the floor.

"Let me try!" Fritz shouted. He grabbed the Nut-cracker with both hands and placed a large chestnut in its mouth. Unfortunately, he pushed too hard on the handle. The chestnut cracked—but so did the poor Nutcracker's jaw!

"Oh, no!" cried Marie, who was very softhearted. She took the Nutcracker from her brother and gently touched the soldier's wobbly jaw. "You poor thing!" she sighed.

Fritz, bored by a toy that broke so easily, went back to his soldiers. But Marie held the Nutcracker tenderly, and wrapped a ribbon from her doll's hair around his broken jaw. The adults smiled at the sight of little Marie trying to mend the broken toy.

Before long the guests departed and the children were bundled into bed. Frau Stahlbaum insisted that the children leave their new toys under the Christmas tree. "You can play with them in the morning," she said.

Late that night Marie awoke and crept downstairs to the parlor to see her beloved Nutcracker. There he was, standing bravely under the glittering tree, sword in hand—but Marie could hardly believe her eyes: the Nutcracker's jaw was no longer broken! "Who fixed you, little Nutcracker?" she whispered softly.

At that moment, the grandfather clock ground and whirred, but for some strange reason, did not strike the hour. Marie looked up and saw that the big, golden owl that usually sat on top of the clock now looked strangely like Herr Drosselmeier.

This frightened Marie and she turned to go. Suddenly, something strange and horrible began to happen. Up through the cracks in the floor and walls came an army of squeaking, scurrying mice! They darted about madly, forming squadrons as neat and orderly as any that Fritz had made with his toy soldiers. Rows of mice blocked the door, so Marie quickly scrambled to a dark corner. There she watched to see what would happen next.

A moment later a horrible creature with seven mouse heads wearing seven shiny crowns came crashing through the wall. He was the Mouse King—ruler of all the mice. Each of his heads was hissing and screaming. They made an awful sound as they chanted:

"The Mouse King is ready to fight!

Prepare, Nutcracker, for battle tonight!"

Having sounded his battle cry, the Mouse King motioned his army of mice to begin marching. Scared, but curious as well, Marie watched them move swiftly forward. Then, all of a sudden, her own dear Nutcracker strode out from under the Christmas tree. With his sword held high in the air, he shouted:

"Whack, whack, whack!

Cowardly mousey pack!

Death shall I bring

To the wretched Mouse King!

Attack! Attack! Attack!"

"Oh, no!" Marie whispered to herself. "They're going to have a battle, but my poor Nutcracker is impossibly outnumbered!" Just then a legion of Fritz's toy soldiers came marching out to join the Nutcracker, and the battle began!

Sugarplums burst out of rifles as the soldiers fired them into the thickest part of the mouse army. Mice fell by the dozens. The Nutcracker then ordered the biggest cannons into position on Frau Stahlbaum's footstool. *Boom, boom, boom!* A flying wall of hazelnuts blasted forth, toppling the mice in droves.

All the while Marie stayed crouched in her corner, frightened, but sure nonetheless that the Nutcracker's army would win. The trouble was, more and more mice kept joining the fight. No sooner did one troop fall than another sprang up in its place. They would promptly gather the silver sprinkles from the Christmas cakes, load their muskets, and begin to fire.

The Nutcracker fought bravely. Soon, however, two enemy riflemen seized him by his wooden coat and hit him on the head. The Nutcracker's sword fell from his hand and went skidding across the floor, and the Nutcracker fell backwards in a daze.

Both armies stopped their fighting and looked at the Mouse King. "Ha!" he exclaimed in his seven scratchy voices. "I've got the Nutcracker now!" He was filled with wicked delight. "He's all mine," he cackled, turning his seven heads to face Marie, "unless someone wishes to help him."

"Wh-what can I do to save him?" asked Marie in a shaky voice.

"Give me all your best candies," said the Mouse King greedily.

Marie crept slowly under the tree, until her hand found the box where she had put all of her favorite candies. Trembling, she

gave the Mouse King seven flower-shaped bonbons, a cat carved out of marzipan, and a handful of delicate chocolate truffles.

"Hee, hee, hee," the Mouse King snickered, seizing the sweets. Marie turned away so that she would not have to see his seven hissing heads as they gobbled up her candies. It made her sad to give them up to something so evil.

"The candy was good," said the Mouse King when he had finished, "but not good enough. You must give me your best toys, too."

Marie turned pale in alarm and anger. How could she give the wretched Mouse King all of her beloved toys? Yet she wanted the Nutcracker to live. With great reluctance she did as the Mouse King asked.

"Heh, heh," the Mouse King rasped, as he took her shepherdess doll, her stuffed bear, and her little wicker baby carriage. "Now, give me your new doll and I'll be satisfied."

But this was more than Marie could bear. "I will not!" Marie cried, stamping her foot. "What will you want next, you horrible creature?" Little Marie was so angry that she took off one shoe and threw it at the Mouse King with all her might.

Stunned, the Mouse King tottered and fell, his seven heads hitting the floor. This commotion jarred the Nutcracker awake. "Quick!" he called to Marie. "Please, bring me my sword!"

Marie dashed over to the Nutcracker's sword, picked it up, and brought it to him. Lit by the full moon shining through the window, the sword flashed like lightning in the Nutcracker's hand. He jumped to his feet—and not a minute too soon, for the Mouse King had recovered from his blow.

The two armies moved aside, and the Nutcracker and the Mouse King began to duel. *Swit! Slash! Swit!* went their swords. The Mouse King was a ferocious fighter, but in the end the Nutcracker had the advantage of having only one head: while three of the mouse heads were arguing over the best next move, the Nutcracker was able to strike the final, fatal blow.

As the Mouse King fell to the floor, Marie burst from her corner to hug her little Nutcracker. But as she did so, he disappeared in a puff of smoke—and in his place stood a handsome, young prince.

"Thank you! Thank you, my lovely Marie!" said the prince, going down on one knee. "I have been under the spell of the wicked Mouse King for many years. Your bravery and loyalty have set me free at last!"

The prince then removed the crowns from the Mouse King's seven heads. Kneeling before Marie he said, "Please accept these tokens of victory from your true and faithful knight." Marie was quite honored to accept the tiny crowns from him.

"Now, to show my gratitude," the prince said, "I would like to take you with me to my kingdom." And with a wave of the prince's hand, a shimmering light poured over them. The Stahlbaum's parlor vanished and a beautiful land spread out before them.

They saw the sparkling and many-colored walls and towers of intricately designed buildings, and the sweetest, most delicious aroma filled the air. "Mmm!" sighed Marie. "It smells like cinnamon and chocolate and peppermint!"

The prince smiled. "That's because this is the Kingdom of Sweets!" he said.

Marie marveled at the splendid arched gateway before her, which was made of macaroons and candied fruits. Walking through it into the town, she saw houses decorated with delicate patterns of spun sugar. Alongside the little streets ran streams of thick, foamy custard, which could be scooped up with a big spoon.

All about, beautifully dressed townspeople were laughing and singing.

The prince led Marie onward, until they came to a castle with a hundred shining towers. Its sugary walls glistened like jewels in the sunlight. "This is the Marzipan Castle," the prince announced as they entered.

Lovely music floated through the hallways, and from one room Marie heard merry peals of laughter.

"Come!" said the prince. "Let's go there!"

In the room were four little ladies, each so exquisitely dressed that Marie was sure they were princesses. Catching sight of Marie and the prince, they immediately jumped out of their chairs and ran to them.

"Oh, dearest prince! Beloved brother!" the ladies exclaimed, for they were his sisters. They embraced him with tears of gladness in their eyes.

The prince wiped away his own happy tears and took Marie by the hand: "This is Marie Stahlbaum," he told them. "It is she who rescued me from the Mouse King's spell!"

The four princesses fell upon Marie, weeping with joy and expressing their heartfelt thanks.

The princesses prepared a banquet in Marie's honor. Marie and the prince sat at an elegant table, with tea, fruits, nuts, and sweets piled high before them. The Nutcracker prince regaled his sisters with the story of his terrible battle against the Mouse King. After they had eaten, two of the princesses sang for them, while two others danced.

Although Marie had never enjoyed herself so much, she found it harder and harder to pay attention. The princesses' voices seemed to be getting farther and farther away from her. She could not even hear her own dear Nutcracker prince. A silvery mist began to rise all around her, and it seemed as if the princesses, the Nutcracker prince, and she herself were all floating, rising higher and higher, until . . .

With a *poof!* Marie fell from a great height. It was quite a landing. When she opened her eyes, she saw that she was in her own bed! It was broad daylight, and her mother was standing at her bedside.

"That was quite a sleep you had," she said. "Breakfast has been ready for hours!"

"Oh, Mama!" Marie exclaimed. "I've just been to the most wonderful place!" And she told her mother all about the Nutcracker prince and the Kingdom of Sweets.

"What a lovely dream you've had, Marie! But now you must get up. It's Christmas morning!"

When her mother had left the room, Marie lingered in bed for a moment, looking around thoughtfully. "Perhaps it *was* just a dream," she sighed, and threw back her covers.

As she stood up, a tiny gold ring slipped out of her nightdress pocket. "What's this?" she cried.

She held it up and drew in her breath. Quickly, she reached back into her pocket and pulled out six more just like the first. Why, they weren't rings! They were the crowns from the seven heads of the Mouse King!

Looking at the miniature crowns in her hand brought back every magical moment she had spent with the Nutcracker prince. And that was the best Christmas present ever!

THE NIGHT BEFORE CHRISTMAS

Clement C. Moore

Twas the night before Christmas,
     when all through the house
Not a creature was stirring, not even a mouse;
The stockings were hung by the chimney with care,
In hopes that St. Nicholas soon would be there;
The children were nestled all snug in their beds,
While visions of sugar-plums danced through their heads;
And mamma in her kerchief, and I in my cap,
Had just settled our brains for a long winter's nap,—
When out on the lawn there arose such a clatter,
I sprang from my bed to see what was the matter.
Away to the window I flew like a flash,
Tore open the shutters and threw up the sash.
The moon, on the breast of the new-fallen snow,
Gave a lustre of midday to objects below;
When what to my wondering eyes should appear,
But a miniature sleigh and eight tiny reindeer,
With a little old driver, so lively and quick
I knew in a moment it must be St. Nick.
More rapid than eagles his coursers they came,
And he whistled and shouted and called them by name;
"Now, Dasher! now, Dancer! now, Prancer and Vixen!
On, Comet! on, Cupid! on, Donder and Blitzen!

To the top of the porch, to the top of the wall!
Now, dash away, dash away, dash away all!"
As dry leaves that before the wild hurricane fly,
When they meet with an obstacle, mount to the sky,
So, up to the house-top the coursers they flew,
With a sleigh full of toys,—and St. Nicholas too.
And then in a twinkling I heard on the roof
The prancing and pawing of each little hoof.
As I drew in my head and was turning around,
Down the chimney St. Nicholas came with a bound.
He was dressed all in fur from his head to his foot,
And his clothes were all tarnished with ashes and soot;
A bundle of toys he had flung on his back,
And he looked like a pedlar just opening his pack.
His eyes how they twinkled! His dimples how merry!
His cheeks were like roses, his nose like a cherry;
His droll little mouth was drawn up like a bow,
And the beard on his chin was as white as the snow.
The stump of a pipe he held tight in his teeth,
And the smoke it encircled his head like a wreath.
He had a broad face, and a little round belly
That shook, when he laughed, like a bowl full of jelly.
He was chubby and plump,—a right jolly old elf—
And I laughed when I saw him, in spite of myself.
A wink of his eye and a twist of his head
Soon gave me to know I had nothing to dread.
He spoke not a word, but went straight to his work,
And filled all the stockings; then turned with a jerk,
And laying his finger aside of his nose,
And giving a nod, up the chimney he rose.
He sprang to his sleigh, to his team gave a whistle,
And away they all flew like the down of a thistle;
But I heard him exclaim, ere he drove out of sight:
"Happy Christmas to all, and to all a good-night!"

CHRISTMAS AT THE CRATCHITS'

Charles Dickens

You might have thought a goose the rarest of all birds; a feathered phenomenon, to which a black swan was a matter of course; and in truth, it was something like it in that house. Mrs. Cratchit made the gravy (ready beforehand in a little saucepan) hissing hot; Master Peter mashed the potatoes with incredible vigor; Miss Belinda sweetened up the apple-sauce; Martha dusted the hot plates; Bob took Tiny Tim beside him in a tiny corner, at the table; the two young Cratchits set chairs for everybody, not forgetting themselves, and mounting guard upon their posts, crammed spoons into their mouths, lest they should shriek for goose before their turn came to be helped. At last the dishes were set on, and grace was said. It was succeeded by a breathless pause, as Mrs. Cratchit, looking slowly all along the carving knife, prepared to plunge it in the breast; but when she did, and when the long-expected gush of stuffing issued forth, one murmur of delight arose all around the board, and even Tiny Tim, excited by the two young Cratchits, beat on the table with the handle of his knife, and feebly cried hurrah!

There never was such a goose. Bob said he didn't believe there ever was such a goose cooked. Its tenderness and flavor, size and cheapness, were the themes of universal admiration. Eked out by the apple-sauce and mashed potatoes, it was a sufficient dinner for the whole family; indeed, as Mrs. Cratchit said with great delight (surveying one small atom of a bone on the dish), they hadn't ate it all at last! Yet every one had had enough, and the youngest Cratchits in particular were steeped in sage and onion to the eyebrows! But now, the plates being changed by Miss Belinda, Mrs. Cratchit left the room alone—too nervous to bear witnesses—to take the pudding up, and bring it in.

Suppose it should not be done enough! Suppose it should break in turning out! Suppose somebody should have got over the wall of the backyard, and stolen it, while they were merry with the goose; a supposition at which the two young Cratchits became livid! All sorts of horrors were supposed.

Hallo! A great deal of steam! The pudding was out of the copper. A smell like a washing-day! That was the cloth. A smell like an eating-house and a pastry cook's next door to each other, with a laundress next door to that! That was the pudding. In half a minute Mrs. Cratchit entered, flushed, but smiling proudly, with the pudding like a speckled cannonball, so hard and firm, blazing in half of half-a-quartern of ignited brandy, and bedight with Christmas holly stuck into the top.

Oh, a wonderful pudding! Bob Cratchit said, and calmly too, that he regarded it as the greatest success achieved by Mrs. Cratchit since their marriage. Mrs. Cratchit said that now the weight was off her mind, she would confess she had had her doubts about the quantity of flour. Everybody had something to say about it, but nobody said or thought it was at all a small pudding for so large a family. It would have been flat heresy to do so. Any Cratchit would have blushed to hint at such a thing.

At last the dinner was all done, the cloth was cleared, the hearth swept, and the fire made up. The compound in the jug being tasted and considered perfect, apples and oranges were put upon the table, and a shovelful of chestnuts on the fire. Then all the Cratchit family drew round the hearth, in what Bob Cratchit called a circle, meaning half a one; and at Bob Cratchit's elbow stood the family display of glass—two tumblers, and a custard-cup without a handle.

These held the hot stuff from the jug, however, as well as golden goblets would have done; and Bob served it out with beaming looks, while the chestnuts on the fire sputtered and cracked noisily. Then Bob proposed:

"A merry Christmas to us all, my dears. God bless us!"

Which all the family re-echoed.

"God bless us every one!" said Tiny Tim, the last of all.

POEMS FOR CHRISTMAS

THE BELLS

Hear the sleighs with the bells—
    Silver bells!
What a world of merriment their melody
    foretells!
How they tinkle, tinkle, tinkle,
    In the icy air of night!
While the stars, that oversprinkle
All the heavens, seem to twinkle
    With a crystalline delight
Keeping time, time, time,
    In a sort of Runic rhyme,
To the tintinnabulation that so musically wells
    From the bells, bells, bells, bells,
    Bells, bells, bells—
From the jingling and the tinkling of the bells.
                    —*Edgar Allan Poe*

22

AS JOSEPH WAS A-WALKING

As Joseph was a-walking
 He heard Angels sing,
"This night shall be born
  Our Heavenly King.

"He neither shall be born
  In house nor in hall,
Nor in the place of paradise,
  But in an ox-stall.

"He shall not be clothed
  In purple nor pall;
But all in fair linen,
  As wear babies all.

"He shall not be rocked
  In silver nor gold,
But in a wooden cradle
  That rocks on the mould.

"He neither shall be christened
  In milk nor in wine,
But in pure spring-well water
  Fresh spring from Bethine."

Mary took her baby,
  She dressed Him so sweet,
She laid Him in a manger,
  All there for to sleep.

As she stood over Him
  She heard Angels sing,
"Oh, bless our dear Savior
  Our Heavenly King!"
     —*Anonymous*

THE LAMB

Little lamb, who made thee?
Dost thou know who made thee,
Gave thee life and bade thee feed
By the stream and over the mead;
Gave thee clothing of delight,
Softest clothing, woolly, bright;
Gave thee such a tender voice
Making all the vales rejoice?
  Little lamb, who made thee?
  Dost thou know who made thee?

Little lamb, I'll tell thee;
Little lamb, I'll tell thee;
He is called by thy name,
For He calls himself a Lamb;
He is meek and He is mild,
He became a little child.
I a child and thou a lamb,
We are called by His name,
  Little lamb, God bless thee!
  Little lamb, God bless thee!
  —*William Blake*

SANTA CLAUS

He comes in the night! He comes in the night!
    He softly, silently comes;
While the little brown heads on the pillows so white
    Are dreaming of bugles and drums.
He cuts through the snow like a ship through the foam,
    While the white flakes around him whirl;
Who tells him I know not, but he findeth the home
    Of each good little boy and girl.

    His sleigh it is long, and deep, and wide;
        It will carry a host of things
    While dozens of drums hang over the side;
        With the sticks sticking under the strings.
    And yet not the sound of a drum is heard,
        Not a bugle blast is blown,
    As he mounts to the chimney-top like a bird,
        And drops to the hearth like a stone.

The little red stockings he silently fills,
    Till the stockings will hold no more;
The bright little sleds for the great snow hills
    Are quickly set down on the floor.
Then Santa Claus mounts to the roof like a bird,
    And glides to his seat in the sleigh;
Not the sound of a bugle or drum is heard
    As he noiselessly gallops away.

    He rides to the East, and he rides to the West,
        Of his goodies he touches not one;
    He eateth the crumbs of the Christmas feast
        When the dear little folks are done.
    Old Santa Claus doeth all that he can;
        This beautiful mission is his;
    Then, children, be good to the little old man;
        When you find who the little man is.

—Anonymous

BETHLEHEM

A little child,
A shining star,
A stable rude,
The door ajar.

Yet in that place,
So crude, forlorn,
The Hope of all
The world was born.
—*Anonymous*

SONG

Neither in halls, nor yet in bowers
Born would He not be.
Neither in castles, nor yet in towers,
That seemly were to see,
But at His Father's will,
Betwixt an ox and ass,
Jesus born He was;
Heaven He brings us till!
—*From an Old Nativity Play*

THE FRIENDLY BEASTS

Jesus our brother, strong and good,
Was humbly born in a stable rude,
And the friendly beasts around Him stood,
Jesus our brother, strong and good.

"I," said the donkey, shaggy and brown,
"I carried His mother uphill and down,
I carried her safely to Bethlehem town;
I," said the donkey shaggy and brown.

"I," said the cow, all white and red,
"I gave Him my manger for His bed,
I gave Him my hay to pillow His head,
I," said the cow all white and red.

"I," said the sheep with curly horn,
"I gave Him my wool for His blanket warm,
He wore my coat on Christmas morn;
I," said the sheep with curly horn.

"I," said the dove, from the rafters high,
"Cooed Him to sleep, my mate and I;
We cooed Him to sleep, my mate and I;
I," said the dove, from the rafters high.

And every beast by some good spell,
In the stable dark was glad to tell,
Of the gift he gave Immanuel,
The gift we gave Immanuel.

(*Twelfth-Century Carol*)

THE YEAR
SANTA CLAUS
ALMOST OVERSLEPT

I t was Christmas Eve afternoon in the North Pole, the busiest day of the year for Santa Claus and his elves.

Sounds of last-minute hammering and yammering and snapping and wrapping filled Santa's workshop. In one corner elves were checking their lists not once, not twice, but *three* times, to make sure that each child received all the right toys. Several elves were fussing over their handmade dolls, adding color to their cheeks or extra shine to their hair. Still more elves were carefully packing Santa's bag with all kinds of splendid toys.

At precisely five minutes before two o'clock, the biggest, merriest elf of all, Santa Claus himself, looked up from his map of the world and gave an enormous yawn. "It's time for my most important nap of the year!" he announced. The elves immediately fell quiet and listened.

"As you know," Santa continued, "I must be well rested before I set off on my all-night journey. Now, who will wake me when it's time to go?"

Instantly, two hundred hands shot into the air, along with cries of "I will! I will!" Every elf longed for the honor of waking Santa up on *this* particular afternoon.

Santa stood up and looked out at his happy group of elves. He knew each one by name, and he even knew the names of their parents and grandparents before them. At last he pointed to three brothers in the far back. "Elmo, Eli, and Jack," Santa said. "I think you raised your hands first."

The three elves beamed, their smiles stretching from one pointed ear to the other. Oh, it was a proud moment for them!

Elmo, Eli, and Jack followed Santa to his room, while he gave them strict instructions. "You must be sure to wake me at four o'clock on the dot!" Santa said. "Millions of boys and girls around the world are counting on me tonight. If you forget to wake me up—"

"Oh, we won't, Santa! We won't!" exclaimed the three elves. The thought of Santa Claus sleeping through Christmas Eve was too terrible to even think about.

"Very well, then," said Santa, nestling under his fluffy quilt. "I'll see you at four o'clock!"

The grandfather clock in the parlor chimed twice: it was two o'clock. "Let's sit right here by the clock," said Elmo. "That way we could never forget!" Eli agreed, and Jack suggested that they play cards to pass the time.

"Have you lost your mind, good brother?" cried Elmo. "Here we are with the most important job in the world, and you want to play cards!"

Eli chuckled. "Well, don't be *too* hard on him, Elmo," he said. "After all, he *is* the baby of the family!"

Now, if there was one thing Jack could not stand, it was to be called a baby. "I am *not* a baby!" he cried. "I— I only thought it was something to do while we waited."

"That may well be," said Eli, "but I do think we should take our job seriously," and he looked at his older brother for approval.

"Yes," said Elmo. "Eli is right. So, let's just sit here on the couch and watch the clock."

And so the three elves sat . . . and sat . . . and sat. They watched the long, black arm of the clock creep ever so slowly downward; and they listened to the clock's steady tick-tock, tick-tock, tick-tock, which was the only sound in the room.

The three elves yawned.

"I think I'll take a quick nap," said Elmo at last. "Eli, I appoint you to wake me up in fifteen minutes."

"All right," said Eli. But no sooner had Elmo fallen fast asleep than Eli's eyes began to droop as well. Catching himself, he stretched and said, "Why, bless my soul! I could use forty winks myself!"

With that, Eli poked his little brother with his elbow. "I'm going to take a short nap too. I appoint you to wake me and Elmo up in exactly fifteen minutes."

"But what if *I* fall asleep too?" Jack asked.

"You can't! At least, not for fifteen minutes. You can take a nap after that," said Eli. Jack grudgingly agreed, reminding himself that fifteen minutes was not all *that* long.

Yet no sooner had his brothers fallen asleep when poor Jack began to feel awfully tired. He shook his head vigorously, but it did no good. He held his eyelids open with his fingers and looked up at the clock. "Only thirteen minutes to go," he told himself.

Jack did everything possible to keep himself awake. He pinched himself. He shook his legs. He even bit his tongue. But none of it did any good, and soon he was fast asleep like his brothers.

When the grandfather clock struck four, the three elves did not even stir. Five minutes passed. Ten minutes passed.

Meanwhile, outside, the elves in charge of packing Santa's sleigh began to get nervous. "He's usually out here by now," they said to each other. Even the reindeer noticed that something was wrong. Finally, Dancer, the head reindeer, picked up his harness and

trotted over to Santa's house.

Dancer peered in through the parlor window. When he saw the three elves fast asleep on the couch, he tapped his antlers against the pane. He tapped for several minutes, until Jack awoke with a start. He looked at the clock—it was fifteen minutes past four!

"Oh my gosh! Elmo! Eli! Wake up! We're late!" Jack shouted.

Still in a sleepy daze, the three elves scrambled to Santa's bedside. "Santa! Wake up! You're fifteen minutes late!" they exclaimed.

"What's this!" cried Santa. "What happened to my reliable clock watchers?"

"It's Eli's fault!" cried Elmo. "He was supposed to wake me up!"

"No, it's Jack's fault!" said Eli. "He was supposed to wake me and Elmo up."

Santa looked down at Jack for an explanation. The young elf's face was flushed and tears filled his eyes.

"What a baby!" Eli muttered.

Jack bristled and burned and tightened his fists, but he did not look at his brother. Instead, he looked straight up at Santa.

"It's all my fault, and I'm sorry, Santa," Jack said. "I was supposed to wake up my brothers, but I fell asleep too."

He wiped away his tears with his sleeve, and then stood up straight. "But I'll make it up to you," he said. "I'll—I'll clean the workshop every night, all year long!"

"Now, now, that won't be necessary," said Santa. "Fifteen minutes won't make much difference in the long run. You've worked hard preparing for Christmas, and you should be tired. Perhaps you should have played a game to keep yourselves awake."

"That's what I said!" Jack started to say, but Santa motioned him not to interrupt.

"I appointed the three of you," Santa was saying. "You were a team. It's not just Jack's fault—you are all responsible." The three brothers hung their heads.

"Ho, ho, ho!" Santa chuckled. "It was an honest mistake, and this is the best night of the year! Don't be sad. The children will still get their toys. Come along now, and help me get ready. We don't want to lose any more time!"

With the help of all of his elves, Santa was soon ready to go. His eight reindeer excitedly pawed the snowy ground, eager to take flight. "Merry Christmas!" shouted Santa. "Meeerrry Christmas!" From his sleigh, he looked out at his beloved elves who had gathered around to wish him well. They were all cheering, waving, and looking as happy as can be.

Suddenly, Santa saw little Jack. Although the young elf was smiling, his eyes looked most unhappy. Santa could tell that Jack still felt bad about oversleeping.

"Ho, there, Jack!" Santa called. "Why don't you hop on? I need someone to hold the map for me."

Jack blinked. "Me? You want me?!" he exclaimed. The other elves all turned to see who could be so lucky. As Jack made his way through them to the sleigh, Santa said, "This young elf was brave enough to take the blame for himself and his brothers. He's quite a responsible elf, and I need someone like him to help me tonight."

That year was as merry a Christmas as ever. Jack guided Santa through many snowstorms and more than made up for the fifteen minutes Santa had lost. When they arrived back at the North Pole, the tired but happy little elf crawled into bed and did not wake up until New Year's Day. And you may be quite sure that Elmo and Eli never called their little brother a "baby" again!

GOOD KING WENCESLAUS

Christmastime is the season for singing carols. Most of these joyous songs celebrate the birth of Jesus Christ. Santa Claus is also a favorite figure in Christmas songs. One Christmas carol, however, tells of a certain king's kind heart, and the good deed he did one winter's night.

The carol, *Good King Wenceslaus*, is based on a legend about King Wenceslaus of Bohemia, a land in Eastern Europe that is now part of Czechoslovakia. King Wenceslaus ruled from 928 to 935 A.D. and was well loved by his people for his generosity. After his death, he was proclaimed a saint.

The story told in the carol took place on a bitterly cold night on December 26, the day honoring St. Stephen. The moon shone brightly on the deep, crisp, white snow. From inside his palace, the king looked out his window and spotted a peasant gathering firewood. King Wenceslaus felt sorry for the man, who was probably quite desperate to be out on such a night.

"Do you know who that peasant is and where he lives?" King Wenceslaus asked his page.

"Yes," replied the king's good and faithful servant. "He lives a good way from here—at the foot of a mountain, near the forest."

The good king asked his page to bring him meat, wine, and firewood, which he planned to bring to the poor man's house. He smiled at how happy the peasant would be to fill himself on royal food and wine, and warm himself with the king's own firewood.

Out into the freezing, howling wind went the king and his page, bearing gifts for the poor, wretched peasant. The king walked steadily, hardly noticing the cold.

After a while, however, the page could stand no more. "Sir!" he called. "It's so dark and so cold, I cannot go any farther."

King Wenceslaus understood, but he did not want to turn back. Instead he told the page that if he followed along in his footsteps, he would be less cold. The page did so, and it seemed to him that warmth sprang from every step the king made.

The carol teaches us that those who help the poor shall be helped themselves.

THE TWELVE DAYS
OF CHRISTMAS

Text and Tune: Traditional English

On the first day of Christmas my true love gave to me
A partridge in a pear tree.

On the second day of Christmas my true love gave to me
Two turtle doves, and a partridge in a pear tree.

On the third day of Christmas my true love gave to me
Three French hens, two turtle doves, and a partridge in a pear tree.

On the fourth day of Christmas my true love gave to me
Four calling birds, three French hens, two turtle doves, and a
partridge in a pear tree.

On the fifth day of Christmas my true love gave to me
FIVE GOLDEN RINGS, four calling birds, three French hens,
two turtle doves, and a partridge in a pear tree.

On the sixth. . . . Six geese a-laying, (repeat previous ones)

On the seventh. . . . Seven swans a-swimming, (repeat)

On the eighth. . . . Eight maids a-milking, (repeat)

On the ninth. . . . Nine ladies dancing, (repeat)

On the tenth. . . . Ten lords a-leaping, (repeat)

On the eleventh. . . . Eleven pipers piping, (repeat)

On the twelfth day of Christmas my true love gave to me
Twelve drummers drumming, eleven pipers piping,
ten lords a-leaping, nine ladies dancing,
eight maids a-milking, seven swans a-swimming,
six geese a-laying, FIVE GOLDEN RINGS,
four calling birds, three French hens,
two turtle doves, and a partridge in a pear tree.

THE STORY OF THE FIRST CHRISTMAS

THE PROPHETS

"For unto us a child is born, unto us a son is given. . . ."
Isaiah, 9:6

Many years before Jesus Christ was born, his coming was foretold by the prophet Isaiah. His story is written in the Bible.

When Isaiah lived, the world was a troubled place, full of sin, sickness, and suffering. Most people had turned away from God. They no longer believed in him or looked to him for help and guidance.

When God looked down from heaven and saw that the peace and harmony he had created for the world no longer existed, he became both angry and sad. He wanted to punish the people who did not believe in him, but he was willing to give them one more chance.

God decided to send down to the world a man who could go among the people and teach them God's peaceful and loving ways. This man would set an example for all people by his goodness and understanding. The man would be the son of God, and his name

The people of Israel were especially eager for the son of God to come to them. They knew that he would help them live a good and honest life. They also believed that he would deliver them from the misery they endured under the Romans, who had conquered their land.

Like so many others, Joseph and Mary had long awaited the advent, or coming, of their Lord. When they learned that they would be Christ's mother and father on earth, the two were filled with joy. Still, Mary and Joseph kept the coming of the holy child a secret, for they were sure that others would not believe them.

The angel Gabriel appeared to Mary on March 25, exactly nine months before Jesus' birth. To this day many people celebrate the coming of the angel. The celebration is known as the Feast of the Annunciation, which means "the announcement of the advent of Jesus Christ." To many, the angel's annunciation marks the beginning of the story of Christmas.

A SAVIOR IS BORN

Mary and Joseph joyfully awaited the birth of their holy son. The Bible describes how the baby inside Mary grew healthy and strong.

As the baby grew, one of the last of the prophets, Zachariah, foretold the coming of a Savior, whose spiritual light would brighten the paths of all people and guide them in the ways of peace. He said that the Savior would come soon.

But as the day approached for Mary to give birth, an order came down from the Roman emperor, Caesar Augustus. He announced that his government wished to take a count of how many people lived under Roman rule. This required every man in Israel to return to the town where he was born.

The emperor's order meant that Joseph would have to register his name in the town of Bethlehem. This was the birthplace of King David, from whom both Mary and Joseph were descended. Because Mary and Joseph wished to be together when their child was born, Mary agreed to go to Bethlehem with her husband.

Mary and Joseph's home in the city of Nazareth was more than one hundred miles from the town of Bethlehem. To travel such a distance would take many days, so Mary and Joseph set out immediately. It was a long, hard journey: Joseph walked the whole way, while Mary, who was nearly ready to give birth, rode on their donkey.

When Mary and Joseph arrived in Bethlehem, the town was filled with many other people who had also come to register their names. All of the inns and lodgings in Bethlehem were full; and even though Mary was about to give birth, no one had a place for her and Joseph to stay.

At last the couple settled in a small stable, where shepherds and travelers kept their animals. Mary and Joseph did not mind the humble setting, for they were grateful for any shelter. They knew that God was with them and would provide everything they needed for the birth of his son.

It was there, in that lowly stable, among oxen, cattle, and donkeys, where one night Mary gave birth to the holy infant, Jesus. To keep her baby warm and happy, she wrapped him securely in a thin cloth blanket. She then laid him down to sleep in a rough wooden manger filled with straw.

So it came to pass that the promised Savior, Jesus Christ, Son of God, King of the Jews, and Prophet of the Highest—for he is called all these things—was born in an ordinary stable, a place where even the poorest peasant was allowed to enter. The son of God was not born to anyone rich or powerful, but instead to a simple carpenter and his wife.

Such a modest beginning helped Jesus to see the world through the eyes of common people. In later years Jesus would speak of God as the "good shepherd" and compare difficult tasks to "fitting a camel through the eye of a needle." These were everyday images that people could understand. This manner of speaking made it possible for Jesus to spread the word of God to all.

"O little town of Bethlehem, how still we see thee lie!" goes a favorite Christmas carol. Its words describe the wonder of Bethlehem on the night when Jesus was born:

"Yet in thy dark streets shineth the everlasting Light; the hopes and fears of all the years are met in thee tonight."

THE SHEPHERDS VISIT THE BABY JESUS

In the quiet, dark night when Jesus was born shepherds up in the hills kept watch over their flocks of sheep.

It was winter then, and the nights were cold, especially up in the steep hills surrounding the town of Bethlehem. The shepherds were poor men, who wore rough, simple clothes and sheepskin coats to keep warm. Their days were often lonely, for they needed to take their sheep to fields where no one else's sheep were grazing. To pass the time they sometimes played music on crude instruments that they carved out of wood.

As these shepherds sat on the frosty, dark hillside that first Christmas night, the angel of the Lord appeared suddenly in the sky. All over the countryside shepherds fell to their knees in fright. But the angel Gabriel said to them, "Fear not: for, behold, I bring good tidings of great joy, which shall be unto all people."

Then Gabriel told them that a Savior had been born that day in Bethlehem. They would find the holy child, who was Christ the Lord, wrapped in swaddling clothes and lying in a manger.

No sooner had the angel said this when hundreds of angels

burst forth from the heavens and began singing praises to the Lord: "Glory to God in the highest!" they sang. "Peace on earth and good will to all men."

When the angels disappeared, the shepherds came together and said to one another, "Let us go to Bethlehem, and see this wondrous thing which is come to pass, which the Lord has made known to us."

The shepherds hurried down the hillsides with their flocks. They found Mary, Joseph, and the baby Jesus in the stable, just as the angel Gabriel had told them. Because they were poor, the shepherds had little to give to Jesus. Perhaps they gave him a piece of cheese or bread, or a little sheep's wool for a blanket.

But the price of their gifts did not matter. These simple people were the first to see and worship Jesus. And though most people at that time did not think much of the ragged lot of shepherds, God saw them differently.

"He shall feed his flock like a shepherd," the prophet Isaiah had said many, many years ago, when he predicted the coming of Christ. Isaiah meant that Jesus would lead his people to goodness and understanding, in the same way that a shepherd leads his flock to a grassy hillside. Later, Jesus would also be called the "good shepherd."

It was thanks to these simple shepherds that word of the birth of Jesus Christ began to spread. After they had seen and worshiped Jesus, the shepherds left the stable full of hope for the world and praise for God. Soon every village and town for miles around had heard the wonderful news: the Savior had been born. And that is the story of the first Christmas.

*

THE STORY OF THE THREE KINGS

"We three Kings of Orient are;
Bearing gifts, we traverse afar;
Field and fountain, moor and mountain,
Following yonder star . . ."
John H. Hopkins, 1857

In a land far to the east of Jerusalem, three great, bearded men pondered a new and unusually bright star in the sky.

These men had spent their whole lives learning and studying. Their understanding of the world was so great that some people thought they had magical powers, and called them "Magi." Others believed that they were kings because of their fine robes and crowns. The Bible simply calls them "wise men."

As they gazed at the beautiful star, the wise men knew that Jesus Christ, the Savior the prophets had written of, had at last been born. They were sure this star would guide them to the holy child.

A poet named Henry Wadsworth Longfellow described how the three wise men went to Bethlehem to worship the newborn king:

Three Kings came riding from far away,
Melchior and Gaspar and Baltasar;
Three Wise Men out of the East were they,
And they travelled by night and they slept by day,
For their guide was a beautiful, wonderful star . . .

The wise men trusted the star to guide them, and they followed it. The journey was long. But their belief in the star led them to the land of Judea.

Once there, they asked everyone they met, "Where is he that is born King of the Jews? We have seen his star in the East and have come to worship him."

But the people they asked had not yet heard of Jesus. They knew only of one king, Herod, Judea's evil ruler under the Romans.

When King Herod heard about the three royal visitors who were asking about the new King of the Jews, he became worried. He knew that the people of Judea did not like him, but he did not want to be replaced by another king.

Scared that his reign would soon end, King Herod called together his priests and scribes. These men had studied the Bible for many years, and they told Herod that the prophets had long predicted that a new king would one day come to rule all of Israel. This frightened Herod, and he called for the three wise men to come before him.

"Go and search for the young child," King Herod told them. "When you have found him, bring me word, so that I may come and worship him also." But the wise men did not realize that Herod was lying. What he really wanted was to find and destroy the baby that he believed would one day take his throne.

The wise men set out again, faithfully following the star. Finally, twelve days after the first Christmas, the star came to rest directly over the stable where the baby Jesus lay. When the three kings went inside and saw the young child with Mary, they knew at once that they had found the son of God.

The wise men knelt before the baby Jesus and offered him the treasures they had brought from the East. These were gifts of gold and rare perfumes of frankincense and myrrh.

That night, when the wise men went to sleep, God appeared to them in a dream. He told them not to go back to King Herod, who planned to harm the baby Jesus, but to return to their country by a different route. The next day, they did as God had told them, and the evil king never found Jesus.

The three kings were the first men outside Israel to see the new Savior. Until their visit, the only people to know of the coming of Jesus were the Jews, who believed that he was coming to save only them. But the wise men's pilgrimage showed that Jesus had come for all people, whatever land they were from, and whether they were as poor as shepherds or as rich as kings.

CHRISTMAS CAROLS

SILENT NIGHT! HOLY NIGHT!

Text and Tune: Joseph Mohr and Franz Gruber, 1818
Translation: John F. Young, 1871

Silent night! Holy night!
All is calm, all is bright.
'Round yon Virgin Mother and Child!
Holy Infant, so tender and mild,
Sleep in heavenly peace,
Sleep in heavenly peace.

Silent night! Holy night!
Shepherds quake at the sight!
Glories stream from heaven afar,
Heav'nly hosts sing, "Alleluia!"
Christ, the Savior, is born!
Christ, the Savior, is born!

Silent night! Holy night!
Son of God, love's pure light!
Radiant beams from Thy holy face
With the dawn of the redeeming grace,
Jesus, Lord, at Thy birth,
Jesus, Lord, at Thy birth.

WE THREE KINGS

Text and Tune: John H. Hopkins, 1857

We three Kings of Orient are;
Bearing gifts, we traverse afar;
Field and fountain, moor and mountain,
Following yonder star.

REFRAIN:
O-oh! Star of wonder, star of night,
Star with royal beauty bright;
Westward leading, still proceeding,
Guide us to Thy perfect light.

Born a King on Bethlehem's plain,
Gold I bring to crown Him again,
King forever, ceasing never,
Over us all to reign.

(Refrain)

AWAY IN A MANGER

Text: Anonymous   Tune: J.R. Murray, 1877

Away in a manger, no crib for a bed,
The Little Lord Jesus laid down His sweet head.
The stars in the bright sky looked down where He lay,
The Little Lord Jesus asleep on the hay.

The cattle are lowing, the Baby awakes,
But Little Lord Jesus, no crying He makes.
I love thee, Lord Jesus, look down from the sky,
And stay by my cradle 'til morning is nigh.

JOY TO THE WORLD

Text: Isaac Watts, 1719
Tune: Adapted from George F. Handel, 1742

Joy to the World!
The Lord is come;
Let earth receive her King;
Let every heart
Prepare Him room,
And heav'n and nature sing,
And heav'n and nature sing,
And heav'n and heav'n
And nature sing.

Joy to the world!
The Savior reigns;
Let men their songs employ,
While fields and floods,
Rocks, hills, and plains
Repeat the sounding joy,
Repeat the sounding joy,
Repeat, repeat
The sounding joy.

HARK! THE HERALD ANGELS SING

Text: Charles Wesley, 1739   Tune: Felix Mendelssohn, 1840

Hark! the herald angels sing,
Glory to the newborn King;
Peace on earth, and mercy mild,
God and sinners reconciled!
Joyful all ye nations rise,
Join the triumph of the skies;
With th'angelic host proclaim,
Christ is born in Bethlehem.

REFRAIN:
Hark! the herald angels sing,
Glory to the newborn King.

Christ, by highest heaven adored,
Christ, the everlasting Lord,
Late in time behold him come,
Offspring of a Virgin's womb.
Veiled in flesh the Godhead see!
Hail, the incarnate Deity!
Pleased as Man with man to dwell,
Jesus, our Emmanuel

(Refrain)

Hail, the heaven-born Prince of Peace!
Hail, the Sun of Righteousness!
Light and life to all he brings,
Risen with healing in his wings.
Mild he lays his glory by,
Born that man no more may die,
Born to raise the sons of earth,
Born to give them second birth.

(Refrain)

WE WISH YOU
A MERRY CHRISTMAS

English Traditional

We wish you a merry Christmas,
We wish you a merry Christmas,
We wish you a merry Christmas,
And a Happy New Year!

Good tidings we bring,
To you and your kin.
We wish you a merry Christmas,
And a Happy New Year!